THE PACIFIC NORTHWEST POETRY SERIES

Linda Bierds, General Editor

OTHER BOOKS BY NANCE VAN WINCKEL

VISUAL POETRY

Book of No Ledge (Pleiades Press, 2016)

POETRY

Our Foreigner (Beyond Baroque Books, 2017)
Pacific Walkers (University of Washington Press, 2013)
No Starling (University of Washington Press, 2007)
Beside Ourselves (Miami University Press, 2003)
After a Spell (Miami University Press, 1998)
A Measure of Heaven (Floating Bridge Press, 1996)
The Dirt (Miami University Press, 1996)
Bad Girl, With Hawk (University of Illinois Press, 1987)
The 24 Doors: Advent Calendar Poems (Bieler Press, 1985)

FICTION

Ever Yrs (Twisted Road Publications, 2014)
Boneland (University of Oklahoma Press, 2013)
Curtain Creek Farm (Persea Books, 2001)
Limited Lifetime Warranty (University of Missouri Press, 1997)

The Many Beds of
MARTHA WASHINGTON

Nance
VAN WINCKEL

LynxHousePress
Spokane, Washington

FIRST EDITION

Cover Art: Presiding, collage by Nance Van Winckel.
Author Photo: Rik Nelson.
Book and Jacket Design: Christine Holbert.

LYNX HOUSE PRESS books are distributed by the University of Washington Press, 4333 Brooklyn Avenue NE, Seattle, WA 98195-9570.

LIBRARY OF CONGRESS CATALOGING-IN-PUBLICATION DATA is available from the Library of Congress.
ISBN 978-0-89924-181-4

CONTENTS

I

II

III

IV

V

It's neither the horror of the white sunset nor the sickly dawn that the moon refuses to illuminate, but rather the sad light of dreams where you float dressed in sequins, O Republics, Defeats, Glories!

—Max Jacob, "Declamatory Poem"

I

AT THE STREAM WITH MAX JACOB

I'd gone with him a few steps into the icy water
because he'd asked. The cold was supposed
to stop. *Soon,* he said.

                     The stream ran through
an engraving still in progress. Red-tipped
burnishing tool—the hum and sear,
          the scorch where our stream drifts
               into estuarial landscape.

                      And my knowing the engraver
                didn't make a speck of difference,
         didn't change the stream's ripples into figments.

Nor, said Max, would our collaborative prayer
        white out Christ's face emerging from a wall
            in 1909 when he was still a Jew . . .
               as he was again, through no
                   wish of his own, dying
             with the yellow star
         sewn to his sleeve
in the Drancy Camp, in 1944.

WHO WAS I TO SAY? WHO WAS I TO CHOOSE?

I kissed the one who most
needed kissing, the one with five
shades of eye-shadow, he who
was almost she, or had the eyes
just been sweetly bruised?

How deep was I buried in the kiss?
Or how far under the many shades
closing across our lids?

Soul-kiss, someone might say,
not yet knowing who nor what's
made up or how hard-earned
the hard-pressed goodbye
going, going, gone between
a newly opened vault of lips.

DAILY CONSTITUTIONALS

Widows walking. Speaking of two old orchardists
at rest at last in the cherry-wood coffins each
had made for the other. The women get to one
end of Main and turn into the wind. Me too,
taking their lead. I follow them up Avenue
of Liking Better What's Still Around to Like.

They step slowly as if trailing packhorses behind them.
They're going to concentrate awhile on their strides
and then not. As I amp up and breeze past,
they're recalling a boy whose amber eyes
they'd tried as girls to match to pebbles
brought home from a canyon, kept in a box, and
will, later today, be affixed above the glued-down,
hand-painted macaroni shells of saint somebody's beard.

I HAD MY REASONS,

e.g., so weary from my own bellyaching, I fell off
      the edge of the third drink, the second dessert, & was
           provoked to more dancing & necking
               & but a shameful tuppence I tossed
                   to the pauper, & I confess
the migraine made me lose track of time,
      the gut cramp had me on another line
           after the ill-advised trade of this tit
               for that tat, which got me stuck
in the last millennium's traffic, where Proust honked
      & peered & peeped, thus exacerbating
           the past-life trauma of being ground
               into a too-white flour, baked into a dough,
                   rejected, & sent back to Ecclesiastes,
where I was deemed not purely enough bred &
      consequently left off the ark, which is why
           I'm late & why I'm in no way
               & no how to blame.

PROUST

You need to rest, I tell Volume III,
laying it open, pages down,
on the arm of the couch.

And from there, its long sigh issues
through me. Week in, week out,
we've cleaved to one another,

and now the consequences of all
we've wrought upon the world
gather in potent storm gusts.

Secrets face down secrets—
each sorrow without a wisp
of "sorry" in it, and no one

here a stranger anymore
to the end coming 'round
as the wild willed out.

THE WILD WILLED OUT

When all the gallivant's gone, you can still steer a way home.

However asleep the town seems, its machinery frolics on,
burping green smoke, roiling in your rearview.

To have lived so long as a verb—*get & go, duck & dive*—
tonight, for once, may the town lie down
through the valley of you.

PAST LIFE READING: SETTING OUT WHEN THE RIVER'S HIGH

None of the final missives you'd received was meant to be read alone. To be read indoors. You'd pledged to leave no wake, make no wounds. A little lie-down in snow, and how quickly your angel became dusty shadow, then grimy sludge, and finally a teensy part of the huge swiftness beneath you, hurtling you—as angels are wont to do—towards the rapids.

MY GUN

Just as I think, Cripes, I'm scared & need
a big dog & feel nearly done with it all,
someone puts a gun in my hand. I hate it
but hold it for a minute anyway—recalling
how I'd sworn never to wear my mother's
mink, but then she made me try it on,
and oh, the warm dense nest of it,
and me as its snug little egg.

I want to give back the gun but my hand
balks. It's already turned the barrel
in the direction of a loathed street light
and my mind's already blown the bulb's
brains out and is now assembling every
speck of awfulness from my 'effing oeuvre,
where the gun's aimed for the worst spots,
which once I believed were the vital organs.

The gun knows. Knows that it is in fact
terribly sad, alone, and only ever loved
badly. And sensing that now, the fearful,
nearly-done-with-it-all one
        lets the all fall away,
                hears herself tell herself
                        to Go On, Drop The Gun
                                and watches herself obey.

BEEN ABOUT

The rat traps emptied, the grain troughs filled.
The distance between sheep shed
and my own ice-melt dripping on the mat
equals the diameter of moonlight squared
on his face as he looks up
and finds me again. Says
he's sure I'd been swallowed
by the elements, says he'd been
about to come looking. I step into
the warm. Two baas from out back
where I'd worked. Two tufts of wool
he lifts from my hair. In just
such a manner are sleek blue words
slyly acquired by a wispy
whiter-than-snow page. He's seen it
happen. Seen a tear of mine, then two,
well up and slip loose
as the little boat of orgasm
veered into the vortex.

I STAND WITH THE CHILDREN

Rain pocks it, then ends it:
the crust of ice the lake wore
for a week. Amid the drops
I stand with the children
on the rocky shore, our
sharpened skates dangling
from our hands. We had an
idea of ourselves out there:
dead center of the lake's eye,
center of the figure eights
we'd each cut: clear and
dazzling in the mind.

II

ONE EYE OPENS

Dear Tomas, the towns pass—slow ones
        and quick magenta ones, and gradually
                the whole Midwest.

The conductor repunches my ticket.
        States fall out, white dots to the floor.

Sleep, wake; sleep, wake
        all the way to Whitefish
                and 1 A.M.,
and in the window a stern woman's face—
        my nose, my pale creased chin.

And the scratch on the cheek?
        No, a mar on the glass.

The chill air of a distilled future
        awaits . . . when my arm is taken
                and my valise and I are helped down.

                Whitefish, Montana. 1:08 A.M.
                    Empty platform. Light rain.

PECKING AFTER

I gauge my manner for the day by the turkeys'. If the day blows a fierce wind (like today), the turkeys stay high up in their pine tree roosts. The trees thrash and lunge about, and the turkeys hang on. *Their* branches, I keep thinking; their claws wrap all the way around. But if it's a day begun by an earthquake (like Sunday), the turkeys must debate the End Times, loudly, and atop my roof. Whichever one exclaims most vehemently *{We must now wander the just-mowed field!}* also stomps.

> I wander the just-mowed field in a thought
>> that stretches to the downed-place in the fence,
>>> one leg of my body of thought
>>>> slipping through, then the other.

ROME: DEENA READING

God causeth the vapor and crenellations
of white foam over the water. And sadness
in my friend's heart, for which she carries
a small card printed with the ten steps

toward the panic exit. She knows them
by heart but reads them again,
squinting, wishing to distill
into a sweet plume rising from a stew.

The card goes back to its slot amid the coins
and cash. She chooseth now to sigh
rather than read. It's a lot of pressure to believe
there's a fountain. Even as we stand by it—

the sputter Keats drank from during those days
he was slowly dying but lingering long enough
to ink a last bright bird into an ode,
his left hand clamped to the cup.

PAST LIFE READING: RECORD KEEPING

And when the house is finally opened and the tomb of records found, note the cuneiform numerals marking important dates of some former history that held you.

Note: we can't say when; their numbers are not *our* numbers. Back then the embrace of red stone was immense. You were a carrier.

LOYAL ORDER OF

Butte, Montana, 1927

The sky's traffic is cumulus, but not too.
Our elk's an arch across Main. Eighty feet high
and just as wide. Beneath its copper-gilded withers
pass boys with tubas, teen twirlers, wreathed
ponies, and the miners' widows—in turn
and on time. Elk of extended thanks.
Darkness adorns those antlers long before
it decks us. Raucous was the way up the Great
Divide; raucous the way down, past the ore-carts,
past the blind mules dozing on their feet.
Dear elk, mayn't we dote awhile longer?
We do it so well from below. March we tall
toward the short story's end. We were all
you withstood. So toots the piccolo.

NEW YORK ⇨ SEATTLE

Heading into unbreakable cloud piñatas
in the good-crazy clock-world,
we go back in time, allowing
the kissing teens in the seats ahead
to seal a deathless past and enter
the next one as ALIVE & IN-LOVE,

which should but doesn't slink behind
in the contrails of an empire failing
by an ongoing optimism spoken with
a hand over a heart, all lingering a bit
on those locked mouths so ahead but
fading into the future past, this cargo
more now than we've been or will be
as we land upon our land.

MARTHA WASHINGTON SLEPT HERE

Between my future bed and any prior
one of hers, sunups may appear as nosebleeds
across the mountain's face. She, me—we watched
as long as we could, then lay tucked beside
our smooth talkers. Under bright duvets
depicting flowery new centuries.

She had her losses and kept mum.
A horse's mane might be shorn
or a swan's wings notched. Martha,
you would be called Marty in 2018.
You would have acrylic fingernails,
tattooed eyebrows. You'd shun meats.

I arrange a bouquet of fall leaves
and golden grasses. Bless this vase
that anchors our slow shared hour
through a gale of years. Time to bank
the fires, reset the silver for our late-comers.

If the swans fly at all, they won't
fly far. Dear Mother of Petticoats, Sister
of a Suede Glove, let our gravy boats pass
in the hall. May my houses go on
going up wherever yours come down.

STILL WITH OUR INDOOR VOICES,

we step outside and greet
the mountain we'd come so far
to see. We were the people
People magazine had never
heard of: sleeping on lawn-chair
cushions in the back of a truck.

Hushed by first light. As if we'd fled—
had we?—a colony collapse.
The no-fire. The in-love
with how a rock cliff
allows the mountain sheep
to dance along its promontories.

The lowlands with everyone we knew
behind us. Our feet blue
from the cold. But we have socks.
Socks of a darker deeper blue.
I hold to you and you hold
to me. We put on the socks.

EVENING PROTOCOLS

Tokens of white stones. A servant girl
arranges them as an open hand atop a hill.

Bats fly up from the well. She fills the jugs
there anyway. The jugs fill the guests' goblets.

Some flounce in her apron's bow will be
her most remembered gesture, not

that far-off hill's bold salute to a dim star,
not her taking her time

snuffing out the candles in each
of the long room's many windows.

THE POWER MAY BE RESTORED

I'm asked to teach a second language while speaking in a third, and Absolutely NOT is, apparently, an unacceptable reply.

The requester flashes a demure smile. *It might be hard at first,* she says, *but it'll get easier.*

We'd entered through a broken cellar door. Standing shivering in the dank classroom feels like blinking awake in a tomb. And maybe, I think—taking the chalk she hands me—maybe that's exactly what's happened, and where.

Pretty, pretty please, her lips pout.

I don't know the second language. Nor the third. Still, the chalk in my fingers takes so naturally to its old friend the slate.

Scritch-scratch, there appears my white answer, which we both bend and squint to read . . . a stark sentence aglow in the new alphabet.

IF WE'RE NOT SNORING, WE'RE NOT SLEEPING

It can't stay the new century long.
Hailstones tamp it down. Pity
for the unhoused comes in waves.
Turned-over shopping carts become
forts . . . brushed into the scene
with four hairs from a dead cat's tail. Don't
touch the cat. Don't smear the paint.

Buy you me a dirty martini.
Three towns over is how far
we have to travel to be nuts
and unknown. But three is no
problem! We assume we're alive there.
We almost out-sing the jukebox,
our barstools like holes in the gum
where teeth once were, and tongues
trying but failing to stay away.

Outside, a fury of flakes keeps us from
seeing exactly whose hand has slipped
around this snowglobe. And trust me, that's
a hand that can shake! We hit the roof.
Bounce off the walls. Did such euphemisms
mean to keep the dreamed-up us dead
but dancing? Dead and lip-syncing?
Around us, a palm of callused sky closes in.

FUTURE LIFE READING: THE SATELLITE BAR

You will have drinks alone at a bar, your head glazed in the fashion of the day. The bar's view includes hurricanes. Ours. Apparently suffering doesn't enlarge the next life but shrinks it down instead. Your small self on a swivel stool. Far below, winds whip wildly, the same turquoise as your flashing-right-now fat irises.

This is all I'm seeing—that bar, that you swiveling—I'm sorry, I'm tired and a bit thirsty myself. Those highballs shimmer in gold cups. Oh, it seems someone's getting married. No, not you.

You lift your cup—a toast?—a one-more?

I can't see what you see, but it's maybe someone you recognize from ages ago, which is how I recognize you, these days back here in my basement hovel, this very you with a crumpled damp $20 bill in your hand, and "Oh, it's you again," I say and in you come, sometimes even in my sleep as I open the door and there you stand. "Oh. You again."

WHOSE CAT?

He belongs to the woman hanging wet
red sheets. His watching. His matching
cat tongue licking. Belongs down
the block to a girl's voice calling
towards a kit-tee, kit kit, kit-tee.

Cat on an old man's knee
momentarily: half under, for half a sec,
the palsied hand. Whisker kiss.

Cat in a killer's shoe. Cat patrolling
the U S of A night alley.
Piss chambers. Fuck labs.

Cat belongs to the D Street twins.
Belongs to rain's runoff, a hearth
in the mind, and sweet sparrow bone
against the tooth. To the city below the city.
Belongs to the black heart, the eye squint,
the ever-nearing needy paws
of the wolf of us.

RAISING VS. RISING

Beneath the grid of the new city
the old city rises as the water table drops.
The cobbles come up. Quite quaint.
To kick away. Sometimes it's not
funny. You laugh the I-forget-myself
laugh. The umbrella of it opens; friends
crowd under. The world drips off.

The flash of *Walk;* flash of *Don't.*
Watch your feet. Shards of china
dishware: purple roses on golden
stems. Hilarious: the cracked-open
god faces. Nothing whole. Laughing all
the way down. Forget-yourself was how
they took you back, and why.

THE ENDLESS SPIEL OF THE D STREET TWINS

One had half his heart bled away
in the shift of attention between births.
They disremember which one. They sip tall
lattes, say we're either for or against them.

They've been buoyed by brisk winds,
twice bitten by strays, and held once
by their heels over water.

Up ahead it's still the old country:
white walls, smokey windows,
and somebody watching.

They suggest we open our minds
and they'll happily demonstrate
how. They lift tiny rose quartz
knives. They say at the right hour
the cost for such a painless prick
to the very quick of being
is zero, zip, nada, nothing.

HIS DADDY'S BOAT

The boy pissing off the aft
says he'll show me how.

We squint into a sunny blaze
of no fucking way.

Hadn't we made ourselves up
since high noon? And wasn't I one

to do as shown? Happy
to piss a little time away?

Breezes sway. Up was oft
a way we were made.

FIST

Its blow to the kitchen table
makes the many legs jerk.
Body-proprietor to the fist must be
obeyed: when the china trembles
and lips quiver as they sip.

The body thrives in the fist. Orbits
the god-work of greenbacks. It falls
and the cold in the house rises.

The fist bangs barely awake into
right NOW and right HERE.

The body lives on in the fist
even as a lid closes over it
and the ground tightens around it,
even as the eye that saw it last
swells, and the ear that felt it most
hears it hardest: deep in and far down
where sudden winds shift.

THE WAY THE **NOW** IS NOW

The rattle at the trail's end
resembled a shrunken
human head . . .

which apparently causes one
to sit straight up, banging into
2 a.m., with a few stars blinking,

also startled
in the darkness
by the darkness.

ARMY OF ANOTHER

Oh Little Wisdom,
       something will find you, some nose, cold;
          some sound, bark;
             some cough, some *hush now,*
         as a pain went forth to meet the place
     yours was, some vine cut from the gut,
some Juned-up sun, some tread, some mite.

IV

AWAITING THE RETURN FERRY

Balfour, British Columbia

Ghostly echoes of old guffaws from a crowd
who's wise-cracked out. Late morning,
we watch the day get darker, not lighter.
Perched on pilings, gulls bring
few peaceful tidings to shore.

Clear last night but for one snowflake
that fell into our old horse's eye—black pupil
that blinked and took me in, where the cold
had blown open a gold spaciousness. High above,
a lofty dome, and dangling from its apogee
what could only be a soul before it's met up
with the body it'll wear to shreds, to rags
around an old shoe on a step.

I stepped at dawn onto this rickety dock.
I'd been trying to read. From the morning's
earliest scrawls on my notebook pages, all the O's
loomed up: silvery blue pearls.

Now I board with the walk-ons.
We move silently. We've heard about
the storm, and we have a good idea
how rough the crossing will be.

BECAUSE B

Your arrival, admit it, was up
and out of the mud. So what,
here you are. One four o'clock
you walk across the lake.
Its ice creaks: gut syllables,
lingo between fish and fowl.

You'd refused the skates because
a) surely then you'd have to
perform a spin, and b) they could
hurt the ice. You its executioner,
you the handle turning the blade.

YOU TAKE IT FROM HERE

Thousand-year-old dead girl fished from the bog. Sickly queens
in ornate throne rooms. We want the next story before the
this-one's done. Lupine and arias flail for attention
outside an open door. At the edge of thought
a smudge of ink. Legend has it
my great uncle's casket—per
his request—had a window.
Of him, all I recall were white
chapters. Recitations by our misty
river. Wishing for a cut-back on etceteras.
Which I now regret. I had a paper boat then
and was keen to launch it toward the grand infinities.

PAST LIFE READING: WHEREWITHAL

A minute into the play's last scene you, silly you, forgot to breathe. A mistake anyone could make. The set: a train car heading through jagged mountains. The falling snow of actors' lines. Dropping softly. Then silently.

Silly you in the cheap seats leaned forward. A little life inside trying to get out. You thought you knew those lines. Too bad no breath was left to let them loose.

COLD INTERIORS: PAGE 137, *MOBY DICK*

The main sail blows a white hole
into where we've been. Truths out
of Infinity—Queequeg's blue tattoos.

Staring at them, me
and the captain. Metatarsals,
runes rippling.

The captain turns to me.
I shrug. How should *I* know
what they mean?

MYSTERY GUEST

She smokes & eats at the same time.
Her blue lipstick & black nails, her
'daahleeng,' her long time in each
bathroom, as the bread gets broken
with nary a crumb for the polis.

Her sashays down hallways—so
almost us—a sea scum smell still
in her hair. Her damp. So nearly
like us, the more we pour into her,
the more we expect will issue
from her, for example those
fifty ponies our host feels
sure he paid for her
in a dream.

We palm her toothpicks as
keepsakes; her cocktail napkins
we can origami later
into your lion—not one iota larger
than my lamb.

WHAT CITY? WHAT DAY?

I was pushing the gurney
and the doctor walking beside it
kept asking questions of the prone man
who stared back at me as if for help
on a grade school quiz: *Who is our
president? What city are we in?*

Saints stood like stone lions
on either side of the elevator doors.
Going up, I put one palm
over the man's cheek and ear. He'd
failed the questions. White heat
warmed my hand as the floors blurred by.

Then the man touched the doctor's
sleeve. *Please,* he pleaded, *I know
people are starving but don't let them
eat me. I can find the way.
I know the road to the kingdom.*

PONY & PUP

I let them out and they bolt for the deer paths
switchbacking up the hills. The ground frozen,
and the old girl's hooves pounding.
The pup trailing, yipping.

Closing the corral, I see last night's moon
still oozy at the back of the sky's throat.

Where, through the wee hours,
they slept by the gate—small brown dog
beside the mare's white belly—
now the ground at my feet steams.

THE PLACE

At first my aunt set the urn of her husband
among his black books—codes & seals, ships & bridges—
then moved him behind the glass door
on a shelf with the pills and vitamins.

A windowsill seemed a good spot for a while,
but later a wicked joke.

When she lifts him today his bits of bone rattle as they did at the last.

      At the last he hadn't wanted to be waked.
      Not for tea or a chat with his son.
      Awakened, he was eager to hurry back.
      He knew just where in the dream
      and which song he'd been called on to sing.

      The house was packed, the orchestra all
      warmed up. Gaslights in the lobby flickered.

SAND LIZARDS

They do mini-pushups in the shade, then race across the sunnier sand to inspect a sandal. My husband says, *Didn't we used to be like them—not last year but before the mid-Cretaceous?*

Look, I say, *they're already trying on my shoe, but it's at least six millennia too big.*

And so we run out our days the way we run out of limes—with a shrug and a *Sweet-dreams* . . . towards here, right here, where the written account breaketh off.

V

WHO CARES, THE TOUR GUIDE JUST
MAKES IT UP AS SHE GOES ALONG

Here we have a woman known to us only as Lady X.
She worked most of her century to rid the world
of high heels. Fearlessly she ventured forth
among the little dancing-in-circles dogs.

She sent back the diamond-studded dildos that arrive
willy-nilly in the mail, and once, when a big truck,
claiming it could ride up over the fog, wanted her
to want it back, she said NO. No to bug zappers.
To elixirs believed back then to make one ageless.

Notice her stitched-in frown. That get-up's called
a wet suit. We suspect she'd wanted unto death
what she plunged headfirst towards in life
(and hence our clever display): the ravaging river
and this unidentifiable tree with the huge white birds.

FONDUE

A bug in chocolate
and I'm supposed
to eat it,

but it's still wriggling.
Hadn't it just
flown in?

Chopsticks hold it
out to me.
I'm to bend
and bite,

the history
of my life—
a little squirming
amid the sweetness.

HER SHORE

Across her shore's wreckage from a distant country's tsunami, she picks her way. Down the beach: doll arm and doorknob, shoe heel and bike wheel, then a wire basket with four tiny bones inside—from a bird? A foot? More flotsam rides the far-off but ever-approaching waves. Their swoosh and scuttle followed by a here-you-are.

The kelp-wreathed tea tin sits atop a chalk-white shelf—as if in the other hemisphere a kettle's about to hiss, as if horror hasn't yet happened, or won't.

Turn. Walk on. Her shore's point juts into beckoning sunlight, ushering back the dream of walking nude through the great library—high walls of books with a window cut into them. What was beyond that window? *What?* In a few more carefully executed steps, it might come to her.

DOSTOEVSKY IN OMSK

Impossible to survive the winter—
these slim trees, tall and brittle
in their ice-cloaks, at the mercy
of the slightest breeze.

      Was the red streak a fox?
         It stops and stares up.
            Ice inching skyward.

The one alone among the shackled ones
watches. The one alone in the library
of the lone mind. Paging through
cold volumes; do not trust
one thing is like another.

With the sound of several rifles firing,
a quick wind has taken down
      the tallest Siberian birch.
      Though the others stand.
           Alone in white shackles.
           Trembling into May.

ILLUSORY CHILL

It was only noon in the novel—startling
under the nearly midnight tick of the NOW.

Surely love was but a few steps forward
for the woman fishing by the bridge . . .

since the man crossing it has just stopped
to ask her for directions. He peers down.

The moon blinds me as I glance up.
All day: not a tug on a single line.
Yet the uttermost impossibilities tempt.

How beautifully her spectral arm points
to the path that leads to the path. Her mouth,

when truly kissed a hundred pages in, becomes
the cold rapids trembling over red stones.

DON'T LET THE DOG OFF HIS LEASH

The day's news is always eager
to be heard. He's received it
whenever he wakes. News!

He wants to bite the tattooed bird
on the paperboy's bicep. No matter
the boy believes the bird brings
a balm of salvation. Not
if the dog has his way. Not if
his growl garners a wing.

The door opens next
on a girl selling mints.
When the dog smells her happiness
he wants to lick it.

On New Years the bottle rockets
wake him: a bark on either side
of the century.

> Coming fully back to himself,
> he's no longer Charon rowing his keeper
> across the river into the willows' shade,
> where she likes to stare up—cool and calm—
> no longer caring which shore she's on.

PAST LIFE READING:
RETURNING WHEN THE RIVER'S SHALLOW

All the words you read indoors hate you. Hate being cooped up. Outside, there'd be midnight dialogues with Debussy. Outside, a river's fed by blue streams. There words pertain.

Once, you were given the gold ink of your dreams. Its goldenness throbbed in your pen. "Eureka!"

Eureka—a word so insipid the page sloughed it off.

What was crucial to say fell eons ago into deep water. Then came along what by this later life you should be (ha, right!) used to: the heavier heaviness of the oar.

I HELD THE AXE,

knowing it's not
the right tool against
the tulips, the wild blooming
field. But still . . .
still loving its heft.

The blue morpho lowers a wing;
the sky comes down. I could wound
what's wounded me—the blade that's
ablaze. I'm the lengths it would go,
all aim in a tight little palm of promise.

To stay those blooms.
Tulips' petals of tears
in the mind. Or to stand—
a minute? a lifetime?—
as a threat until the threat's passed?

To stand among these
sweet young grasses
just beginning to sprout
over the trouble
and through the heart.

DEAR SIR

Scare Crow, you infidel
in damp traces, in the ripped
shirt of my dead father, you are quite him
at the row's end, but fearless. You, guilelessly
living among seasons, give
back to the rain a burr in that burl of a noggin'.
Oh the centuries it's locked out.

I buy my two ears of corn,
drive off, eat, and die, so maybe by 20?? you'll slip
into my old jeans. Your flung-out arms
outlast everyone's weariness.
You: taking your crow-terror straight. Neat. Amid
all the days and nights of the cuke flowers
nothing's yet burned holes for the eyes.

No doubt he'd grabbed her right from her roost, and that's where he sat now, like a fat brown burl, thirty feet up a fifty-foot pine. From across the ravine I could hear her wings—one, then the other—as they were sheared off and plummeted down. Shrieking, dying, she sounded like a three-year-old throwing a fit. But just for half a minute. Then she was quiet. The white strip of raccoon eyes rose, and I saw the clamped jaw shake the carcass . . . a grisly semaphore.

From under the thinnest husk of a March moon came the staccato clatter of teeth against small bones and the louder snap as he cracked through the ribs. The air was crisply cold. Brief silences followed by showers of feathers. He was taking his time. So was I, shivering out there on the balcony, finishing my smoke in the dark.

ACKNOWLEDGMENTS

Thanks to the editors of the journals in which these poems (some in slightly different versions) first appeared:

American Literary Review: "Past Life Reading: Returning When the River's Shallow," "Past Life Reading: Record Keeping," and "Past Life Reading: Wherewithal"

American Poetry Review: "Daily Constitutionals" and "Sand Lizards"

Cincinnati Review: "Fist"

Connotations: "Mystery Guest"

Crab Creek Review: "If We're Not Snoring, We're Not Sleeping"

Crazyhorse: "One Eye Opens"

Denver Quarterly: "Don't Let the Dog Off His Leash"

Field: "I Had My Reasons"

Gettysburg Review: "At the Stream with Max Jacob"

Gulf Coast: "Rome: Deena Reading"

Hotel Amerika: "Who Cares, The Tour Guide Just Makes It Up as She Goes Along"

The Journal: "Martha Washington Slept Here" (as "Among the Bedlamites"), "Whose Cat," and "Raising Vs. Rising"

Jubilat: "Army of Another"

Kenyon Review: "Loyal Order Of" and "You Take It from Here"

Michigan Quarterly Review: "Pecking After" and "His Daddy's Boat"

Ninth Letter: "Evening Protocols"

Poetry: "Been About"

Poetry Northwest: "Who Was I to Say? Who Was I to Choose," "Proust," "Future Life Reading: The Satellite Bar," and "Past Life Reading: Setting Out When the River's High"

Prairie Schooner: "What City? What Day?"

Referential: "Illusory Chill"

Roger: "Raccoon Eating a Wild Turkey"

Southern Review: "The Place"

The Literary Review: "Dear Sir"

The Talking River Review: "I Stand With the Children"

Third Coast: "The Endless Spiel of the D Street Twins"

West Branch: "The Wild Willed Out"

Willow Springs: "Because B"

Zone 3: "I Held the Axe"

Note: "One Eye Opens" owes a debt to Tomas Tranströmer's poem "Tracks."

THE PACIFIC NORTHWEST POETRY SERIES